2 5 SEP 2015

Nottinghamshire County Council

DP&P(O) 03.10/Comms/4261

County Library

Please return / renew by the
last date shown.

*Blast is dedicated,
in loving memory,
to my dad and my brother Chris*

Blast

Kevin Fegan

www.fiveleaves.co.uk

Blast

Kevin Fegan

First published in 2002 by
Five Leaves Publications,
PO Box 81, Nottingham
NG5 4ER
info@fiveleaves.co.uk
www.fiveleaves.co.uk

Five Leaves acknowledge financial support
from East Midlands Arts

east midlands
arts
making creative
opportunities

ISBN 0 907123 39 2

Typeset by Four Sheets Design and Print Ltd
Printed by Goaters of Nottingham

THE FOUR ELEMENTS

I am consumed by fire,
I am drowning in water,
I am buried in the earth,
I am falling through the air.
Fire, water, earth and air combine
in a sensational act of creation
to produce steel.
A product realised by mankind,
a triumph of our mastery
over the elements,
harnessing mass and energy.
Factories manufacturing factories,
transforming steel into
countless buildings where I live
between Rotherham and Sheffield.
This steel becomes the bridge
I used to cross to go to work,
the ship which took my wife and I
on our honeymoon to Holland,
the tanks and planes that wage war
across the world in our name,
the new car I bought with my redundancy,
the knives and spoons to eat my dinner,
the key to open my front door.
Steel does not exactly breathe
but it has taken its place

alongside the flowers and trees
that harness the sun and the rain,
the earth and the air,
in their own acts of re-creation.
I am consumed by fire,
I am drowning in water,
I am buried in the earth,
I am falling through the air;
but I have nerves of steel.
I have survived these last forty years
of dirt and graft,
the laughter and the sweat,
I will survive a few more years yet
and enjoy this early retirement,
if it kills me.

THE FIVE SENSES

This is iron
and this is steel
and this is the one that will make you squeal.
Eyes, ears, nose, mouth, hands,
the sensational act of creating steel.
The heating and cooling,
the lifting and dropping
of heavy industry
and it doesn't come much heavier than this.
In the melting shop
the roar of the furnace
where solid becomes liquid
and liquid becomes gas,
fired by electricity
in a fierce exchange of mass and energy.
The tapping of molten steel
into giant ladles as this strange
alloy of iron and carbon
is always held at arms' length
while it is shaped into ingots or billets
or whipped and coiled into strips
as it snakes its way through rolling mills.
Truth is, I miss the oily smell
of coolants on hot metal,
the taste of grease in the air,

the drone of electricity
and the pounding of the 10,000 ton press,
its hydraulic legs pumping
like a weightlifter snatching at the bar.
I miss the apparent weightlessness
of enormous furnaces twisting into place
or ladles swinging from overhead cranes
where you could push their terrifying weight
with one single hand.
I miss the finished product
in the machine shop
where lathes, the size of art galleries,
turn and shape turbine shafts
to precision until they shine
like giant pieces of jewellery.
Steel, Peech and Tozer, "Steelos",
it were like a small town.
You name it, we had it; we'd got it made:
our own hospital and fire brigade,
gymnasium, sports stadium,
golf course, tennis courts,
bowling green, football teams,
sports club, social club –
Victor Sylvester and his orchestra
at the annual dance every year.
Brings a tear to your eye
the amount of beer consumed that night.
I've done weightlifting, boxing,
swimming, diving,
archery, hockey, even water polo,
oh aye, we had it all at Steelos.

All that remains are a few battered signs
pointing to an immediate past:
"Hot Metal in Motion",
"Slagging Imminent",
"Famous Last Words".
And what words were those uttered
by the final casualties of this sweatshop,
the men in caps and scarves
like football supporters chanting
for that elusive goal?
My donkey-jacket is still warm
in its locker, that's how quickly
times have changed around here.
1959 was my first year:
15 years old, it was a bit of a shock.
I was a post-boy first-off,
delivering the mail
so I could learn where everything was
and who was running the show.
For five years I served my time
as apprentice plater, reading drawings
and fabricating things out of steel.
I've worked every inch of this place:
top and bottom of furnaces,
up and down chimneys and overhead cranes,
I've been to hell and back again.

WATER

I am drowning in water
and water finds its own level.
The tide swept in behind me
and cut me off from the land.
This is not what I had planned.
I was in a boat with a single sail,
it will be around here somewhere,
there was a sudden gale,
I must have capsized.
I don't know which direction to swim?
I can't tell which way the compass lies?
How much longer can I stay afloat?
I'm treading water,
it's salty in my mouth like sweat.
A white cotton towel
is stuffed into my mouth
to stop the heat from burning my lips and tongue.
My mother did the washing on Mondays:
she boiled the sweat towels white
and hung them out to dry on the line,
one for each day of the week.
My son always complained his grandma
smelled damp like a corner shop.
I remember how the midwife
was bathing our son shortly after his birth
when I came home from work
and she let me hold him in the water

before handing him back to his mother.
I remember looking at my son a while
and thinking how much a simple smile
lights up the human face.
I kissed my wife, cracked some witty line
and cuddled our toddler daughter
to prevent us both from crying.
His sister used to share his bath:
they'd press wet handprints onto the plaster
and splash each other
with uncontrollable laughter.
I taught my children to swim:
they swear I just threw them in,
but I was always there,
keeping them afloat
until such time as they could cope alone.
Before long, they were diving off
the top board without a care in the world,
summersaults, backflips, everything
I never dared to do.
What little I know comes, not from teachers,
but from within:
the instinct in us, as creatures,
is not just to have kids
but to love our kids.
The River Don flows naturally
through the valley:
the water is flashing with sunlight
and sparking like fire.
Where there are mills you'll always find water,
fundamental to the making of steel:

it's water that seals the furnace shut
and cools the lid and cables above,
it's water that drives the hydraulics
on the hammers and forging press
and it's water that spells danger.
It's not the molten steel,
which shares the same fluidity
and behaves similarly,
that is the biggest single hazard
in the mill, nor the huge overhead cranes
or the locomotives shunting along;
but water itself,
simple and fresh from the Don.
When hot metal and water make contact
it's a case of stand well back, if you can,
before the inevitable explosion.
Water runs its sensual course to the sea:
I met my wife at Skeggy,
turns out she lived down the road
from me at Templeborough,
her house backed on to the mill.
I used to slope off from the afternoon shift
and nip over the wall for supper,
then back again in time so as not to be missed;
they'd have sacked me if I'd been caught.
We did most of our courting
by the river, having a right laugh.
We'd sit on the bridge at Forge Island
and I'd sneak a crafty kiss,
we'd write our names on a piece of paper
then fold it into a raft,

make a secret wish
and sail it out to sea.
Once we fell in, she daren't tell
her folks she'd been with me.
Her clothes were so wet I could see
the outline of her body – I treasure
that image of her in my memory.
Water assumes the shape of the vessel
in which it is contained:
we settled down, she took my name,
we enjoyed the same things in those early days.
Her mum and dad gave us a room
until such time as I could provide.
We bought a house nearby
and when she started nesting
I set-to on the d.i.y.,
first with the nursery, then the rest.
I used to lift a few bits and bobs from work,
nothing anybody would miss,
perks of the job. I once built a lean-to
and a little pond courtesy
of Steelos, no one ever knew.
The wife did us proud with a baby girl,
she gave me a daughter then a son,
I was the happiest man in the world.
Life seemed straight-forward, clear.
Suddenly the water turns to beer
and 15,000 men are at the bar
trying to get served.
One by one they collapse
and die of thirst

until there's only me left standing
and the barman asks, "What'll it be?"
and the best bitter tastes very sweet.
I am shaken from my dream
by a siren screaming:
my son is in trouble.
I can see his face bubbling under
the water. At first I think
he's larking about in the bath
with his toys or playing sharks
with his sister at the swimming baths
or hiding behind a waterfall,
pretending he's an explorer;
but then I realise
his face is turning blue, his eyes
are bulging and he's reaching
out for me to rescue him.
I dive under to pull him
to the surface; but suddenly
I'm back in front of the furnace
with the first-hand warning me to stand back,
there's a serious risk of a water splash.

AIR

I am falling through the air;
but what a view:
I can see for miles around
the fairy lights of steelwork towns.
It's an out-of-body experience,
a never-never going to land.
I see the Seven Sisters at Rotherham
and the fourteen furnaces
of Templeborough,
a cathedral of a place,
the biggest melting shop in the world,
more of a village than a foundry.
It's air that puts the blast into blast furnace:
no fire without oxygen, is there?
A lance is lowered into the furnace
for the blow and, simply by fixing his eye
on the white heat, the blower
knows its temperature to the degree.
Once the blast furnace is lit,
it never goes out
for the rest of its natural.
And as I fall,
I am casually airbrushing landscapes
with my oxy-acetylene torch,
adding a few finishing touches to nature.
I am surrounded by electro-magnetic forces,
a paradox of effects and causes
beyond my control.

Any minute now a giant magnet
will swing across and save me,
hoist me back up into the crane
and keep me safe from myself again.
Why am I so attracted to an industry
which has drained my natural energy?
One single electric arc furnace
can use electricity enough to supply
a large town of 100,000 people.
The furnace fills the mill with fumes
from here to eternity,
funny how so much oxygen
results in such filthy air.
We had a cloth cap
and a bit of a nun's veil type-of-thing,
it was all on a wing and a prayer.
Nowadays you see these platers
looking like astronauts with special tubes
fed into the backs of their helmets,
supplying breathing air,
that's what they call it.
My grandad smoked Capstan Full Strength,
the strongest cigarettes known to man,
120 per day.
He had a permanent stain on his moustache,
a kink in his lip
and a reputation for doing things his way.
A bit of red dust from the works
never bothered him.

He was held together by pollution,
fresh air was more of a problem
than a solution.
I tell you what I really hate:
air-fresheners.
Whose bright idea was that?
To fill taxi-cabs with rotting chemicals
spinning on a piece of string
or living rooms with aerosol sprays
or the sticky strawberry smell
in posh urinals – what's all that about?
It's not as if I'm pissing fresh cream, is it?
When I was a child
I used to shoot birds with my air rifle.
It never occurred to me
I could have kept a kestrel,
that there was more to life than industry.
The closest I ever came to nature
was having a crap behind a tree.
Why were ugliness and cruelty
second nature to me?
For years, football was my mission:
chasing a rolled-up bladder covered in leather
became my sole ambition.
There is nothing quite so graceful
as rising like a dancer
to meet a corner kick,
making contact with a flick of the head
and watching the ball fly into the net.
The only thing that could ever compare
was watching our children do better than us.

My son was signed for Sheffield Wednesday:
I love football,
I wanted him to play professional;
but all that really mattered
was keeping him out of the mills.
In the end, he left these green and grey hills
to study near his girlfriend,
thankfully; ask any man,
they'll rage against the north wind
to be with the right woman.
I assumed I had the right one;
but it's never that simple, is it?
I hated being on nights,
I didn't mind the other shifts,
which meant that every three weeks
I was unbearable to my family.
We needed the quids
so I'd take it out on her and the kids.
I was doing my bit,
keeping us going financially,
I didn't see why we had to split.
Job for life, wife for life,
that's the way it's supposed to be.
I was convinced she was seeing someone:
why else would she turn against me?
She knew I'd been unfaithful,
you hope she'll think it's what men do.
Your pride takes a battering 'cause people
know what's happening between you.
There's no secrets in steel,
yet there's no showing how you really feel.

She was gone six months or more,
I was ready to end it all.
She was in a single room at her mum's,
I was living in a vacuum,
then she gave me a second chance.
It was pretty strained; but at least
the pain was bearable.
I did feel ashamed.
There is something in the air we never see:
another energy alongside
ultra-violet or infra-red,
as profound as smell or sound,
as natural as electricity,
as powerful as gravity.
It took me a lifetime to discover beauty:
I never really learned to feel
until I found a beauty in cold steel.

FIRE

I am consumed by fire
like a storyteller who has to tell his story.
Fire, it's sommat you live with, in't it?
You can't think of steel without thinking fire.
Looking into the furnace
is like staring at the sun,
it's the same kind of pain
that makes you lower your eyes in respect.
I've been burned many a time:
arms, legs, fingers, nothing serious.
I've seen my socks stuck to my legs,
I've seen wellies melted onto feet,
helmets melted onto skulls.
I've seen me dad stalking the furnace
like it was a dangerous animal,
walking round it in a circle,
like the platform was his circus,
fettling with his shovels,
towel in his mouth,
the sweat pouring off him.
I've seen a fella throw his entire
wage packet into the fire,
swore he didn't do the job for the money.
I can't for the life of me see why anyone
would put themselves through purgatory
if it wasn't for the money?

Needless to say, he was a single fella
living in lodgings on his own,
I suspect he had no one
to spend his hard earnings on.
Our son was born on a Wednesday
and died on a Wednesday.
Outside the crematorium
lightning flashed across the sky
the day our son died.
Inside we lined up in pews
in front of a furnace,
aware how dangerously close we are
to our own mortality.
Death is so final.
Why did a spark of cancer ignite in him?
It spread like a forest fire
consuming cells faster
than they could be replaced.
It would not be contained,
redirected or extinguished,
it ravaged through his body,
turned his red flesh to a steely grey
and finally reduced him to ash.
We could not save him,
we could only watch him burn.
From diagnosis to death
the whole process lasted
no more than three months,
as if it had been designed,
manufactured and delivered
to a deadline.

It feels unnatural
that my son should die before me.
I deliberately kept him out
of the industry so that he'd be safe.
We encouraged him to live somewhere green
and to see some of the things we'd never seen.
We watched him hold his own children,
and wrap his warmth around them.
His eyes were as blue as our planet
and inside a volcano roared.
He was a source of energy and love,
a force to be reckoned with,
a son and a brother,
a husband and a father,
a man.
He asked me how to die?
And as I cried, I became his son,
the boy to his man.
If you want to know how to live your life,
look a dying man straight in the eyes.
Life is a good fire
around which stories are told
and, in the end, when the fire goes out,
all we are left with are words.
My son spoke to me as I speak to you,
not from wisdom or pity,
but of necessity.

EARTH

I am buried in the earth
with the slag and the scrap and the waste.
I am a blast from the past
with my moleskin trousers and sweat towel,
my wage slips
and Victor Sylvester concert tickets,
my beer vouchers and clogs,
and my job-for-life.
I pass into history
with the Phoenix Social Club,
with Forge Island and Tinsley,
Steelos and Brown Bayley,
Hadfields and Parkgate
and, like all my best mates,
I'm well past my sell-by date.
I'm sitting at a posh table
with as much as a body can eat and drink
and all for free.
The management have splashed out
on a dinner party for the workers
to mark the end
of the Rotherham Melting Shop.
Someone raises their glass and proposes
a toast to the Seven Sisters,
the seven furnaces
forever closed for business.

We might as well be raising our glasses
to Hatchet MacGregor, Thatcher's man;
why don't we just thank our betters
for sacking us and have done with it.
I used to make miniature sculptures
from scraps lying around the shop floor —
motorbikes usually, mini choppers,
it was a way of passing the time.
During the strike
we had to survive off scraps,
it was good practice for the thousands
thrown onto scrap heaps these last 20 years.
I'm walking on the sand-dunes
between Mablethorpe and Skeggy,
it's approaching sunset
and the sun and the moon are both in the sky.
I'm with my wife and kids
and our red setter is running wild.
We've escaped the caravan
to enjoy being a family for a while.
Our son and daughter chase
the dog into the sea,
I can feel the spray on my face;
I pick my wife up in my arms
and spin her 'round in this vast open space.
Steel starts with the earth:
iron ore, wood, sand.
The designers take their paper
and measure shapes to scale,
the pattern-makers turn the paper
into wooden replicas,

then the wood is wrapped in sand
and resin made from cornhusks
to create the hollow moulds
which shape the steel.
Without the earth there is no steel.
For 2000 years, Templeborough
has been a site for production,
now Mother Nature's reclaiming the land.
Look how overgrown the land has become,
you wouldn't even know that steel
had been produced on some of these sites.
Everything comes from scrap
and returns to scrap,
there's no such thing as waste.
I'm at the cemetery
where my wife is laying flowers
at our son's grave.
I've lost the power of speech
and I don't know how to behave any more.
I see her there, a woman
at one with the earth,
allowing herself a chance to grieve,
accepting our son's death
as naturally as she accepted his birth.
I realise I have never thanked her
for our children,
for giving us a son and a daughter,
so I take her in my arms,
spin her gracefully 'round,
smile into her face
and I thank her
for showing me how to survive.

FOUR ELEMENTS REVISITED

No regrets, if I could
do it all over again, I would.
I had to take one last look at the old place.
I suppose I've been keeping the steel warm,
pretending the furnace hadn't gone out,
hoping the works hadn't closed forever,
refusing to accept our son had died.
I was consumed by fire,
I was drowning in water,
I was buried in the earth,
I was falling through the air.
I feel as though a massive charge
of electricity has struck the steel
and magnetised it
and the furnace is finally earthed.
I imagine this giant magnet
lifting the weight off my shoulders,
extracting particles of dust and steel
from my eyes and allowing me to see,
unblocking my nose and ears
to richer smells and sounds,
opening my mouth, releasing my words,
and touching me somewhere deep inside.

I am purged by the fire,
I am floating on the water,
I am embraced by the earth,
I am flying through the air.

"I remembered that when I was small, I used to think there was a dragon in t'steelworks 'cos when the doors opened to let the trains out that were pulling stuff you could see all this red and all these sparks and flames. I used to think – there's a dragon in there – and when they had the arc furnaces all these lights, big bright, white lights if the door opened you could see and think, boy! How did folk work in places like that?"

Lynne Moss

"On that plant, the worst place to work in were the strip pickling plant where they used to put steel strip into an acid bosh – and the stench of acid and that – those that worked there it turned their teeth black. Acid would rot their teeth. Horrible. Horrible place to work – but people used to work there."

Laurence Ford

"Biggest melting shop i' the world – quarter of a mile long – bigger than a cathedral – and that were built in 1917. And there were 14 open hearth furnaces. The furnace – it took a bit o' that, and a bit o' something else an' you keep adding to it – and they used to lift the furnace door and they could tell that's about ready, and they would make a cast. It took 16 hours doing about 80 ton in one cast. Now it teks 55 minutes to do 200 ton. When I was a master cutler in 1995, I was able to say that in the previous year more steel had been made in the Sheffield and Rotherham steel conurbation, than ever in history."

Geoff Burgin

"When I was 18 me brother was in rolling mills at English Steel and he said what do you think? They're setting women in ont' floor. They'd already got women on cranes and little roundabouts. So I went down and got a job. An' I used to work wi' tongs and everything, hot steel. Some t'shops were terrible though, crane drivers learned how to lip-read. We used to leave notes on seats about what were going off in t'shop or if we fell out wi' anybody or if we fancied anybody."

Margaret Barraclough

"...one of the riggers came in an' he says to me – I don't know who's in bottom cellar but they won't survive. A big fireball's just come out o' this end o' cellar and gone straight up into roof. A slag-pot had come up and touched the buffers and t'liquid slag had gone out an' all the ground were saturated in diesel... there were three people fried in that one."

Clifford Heap

Credits

Blast was first broadcast on 18th June 2001 by BBC Radio Drama
Produced and Directed by Melanie Harris
Performed by Paul Copley
Interviews by Clare Jenkins
Music by Ivan Stott

Blast was first performed live on 12th November 2002 at Contact Theatre in association with Manchester Poetry Festival
Directed by Andy Farrell
Performed by David Hobbs
Designed by Andrew Wood
Video by Matt Mawford
Lighting Design by David Martin
Assistant Director: Sam Colling
Stage manager: Lynn Howard

Special thanks to Ric Michael and Ross Bradshaw

Thanks also to Stephen Feber; Katherine Beacon; Helen Riley; Bill Allard; Crowe; Gillian Price; Darren Poyzer; Geoff Burgin; Lawrence Ford; Clifford Heap; Jack Middleton; Lynn Moss; Ally Rodgers; Ralph Temperton; Margaret Barraclough; Ian Nichols; Ian Handley; Daniel Weaver.

Kevin Fegan

Kevin Fegan has written over thirty plays for the stage. His plays for Contact Theatre include *Strange Attractors* about virtual reality, *Excess XS* about the rave scene and *McAlpine's Fusilier* about the Irish in Britain. His site-specific work includes *Lord Dynamite* (with John Fox) for Welfare State International and *Seven-Tenths* for Walk the Plank theatre ship. Two plays about prison life, *Private Times* and *Rule 43* have also been performed in British prisons.

Kevin has written six plays for B.B.C. Radio 4, plus a Woman's Hour serial and a Classic serial. He has also written two short films and worked as a storyliner for Coronation Street. Previous books include *Matey Boy* (Iron Press), an epic poem written and performed by Kevin, based on the lives of shipyard workers at Barrow-in-Furness.

Kevin Fegan recently set up BIG Theatre Company with Director Andy Farrell. Their first production was *52 Degrees South*, about the Falklands War, at the new Imperial War Museum North. His forthcoming radio play, *Racer*, will be broadcast on Radio 4 and published by Five Leaves. Further information is available on www.kevinfegan.co.uk.

Illustrations

The illustrations for *Blast* were taken from a set of slides found in a skip outside the closed down Templeborough melting shop in South Yorkshire. They are from the 1930s. The photographer and workers in the picture are unknown. The full set of slides is now in the archive of Magna – the science centre between Rotherham and Sheffield, built into a redundant steelworks.

Also Available from Five Leaves

I Married the Angel of the North by *Peter Mortimer*
0 907123 293 7, 70 pages, £6.99

Peter Mortimer is a writer whose work spans different ages and cultural divides. In this collection the comic and serious exist side-by-side, performance poetry next to quieter, more reflective work. The poems range from the absurd, to moving accounts of fatherhood, and verse rooted in his adopted North-East.

Peter Mortimer is the unsung hero of Northern literature
NEWCASTLE JOURNAL

The Smug Bridegroom by *Robert Hamberger*
0 907123 88 0, 78 pages, £6.99

A set of deeply personal poems, reconciling the anecdotal and the rhetorical. His writing traces the shifts in family life, break up and renewal.

Robert Hamberger writes in a deceptively simple manner. A must for poetry readers and a perfect introduction for the curious.
GAY TIMES

I've often seen the sonnet as a kind of straightjacket in the wrong hands, but Hamberger makes them fly.
IAN MCMILLAN

Five Leaves' books are available from bookshops or, post free, from Five Leaves, PO Box 81, Nottingham NG5 4ER. A full catalogue is available on www.fiveleaves.co.uk.